To My Dear Friend,
Patricia,
    With Blessings,
    Virgie Buford
        11/19/04

venues
for Success

Also by Virgie M. Binford
with Dorothy N. Cowling

Self-Esteem Enhancers
Inner-Directed Guidelines for Successful Living

Avenues for Success

*Turning Adversity
into Opportunity through
Strong Support Systems*

Virgie M. Binford

PROVIDENCE HOUSE PUBLISHERS
Franklin, Tennessee

Printed in the United States of America

05   04   03   02   01   1   2   3   4   5

Library of Congress Catalog Card Number: 00-109562

ISBN: 1-57736-218-7

Cover design by Gary Bozeman

Providence House Publishers
238 Seaboard Lane • Franklin, Tennessee 37067
800-321-5692
www.providencehouse.com

WHERE THERE IS VISION, THERE IS HOPE.

WHERE THERE IS HOPE, THERE IS FAITH.

WHERE THERE IS FAITH, THERE IS LOVE.

CONTENTS

Preface and Acknowledgments   ix

PART 1   1
  1. Introduction   3
  2. Case Studies   7

PART 2   47
  3. Attributes of Strong Support Systems   49
  4. Reflections on Research Related to
    the Effectiveness of Support Systems
    for Success   55
  5. Examples of Effective Strong Support Systems   67
  6. Reflections   77

7. A Bird's-Eye View of Support Systems
   in Action in South Africa   81
8. Suggestions for Developing a
   Support System for Excellence   87
9. Strong Support Systems   93
10. Conclusions   101

Suggestions   106
Notes   111
Bibliography   113
About the Author   116

PREFACE & ACKNOWLEDGMENTS

 Five decades as an educator and a leader in several professional organizations has afforded me the opportunity to teach, administer programs, and travel to several continents. As an educator, I have observed that most people who succeeded in achieving their goals and objectives were fortunate enough to have support systems of mentoring with faith, hope, and unconditional love.

During study tours, I interacted with many multi-ethnic and multicultural groups. In each contact, I have been honored to meet and greet success-oriented people who testified that they succeeded because of support systems which empowered them to reach the pinnacle of achievement. Their revelations inspired me to share these positive results with readers, as an incentive to seek and find avenues of success by reaching out to those who are willing to share their time and expertise to nurture and challenge others in order to develop their maximum potential.

Many advocates provided me with positive reinforcement that empowered me to achieve my fondest dreams. Counseling, guiding, and strengthening with diversified human and material resources enabled me to overcome obstacles of doubt and achieve many dreams and desires. Caring, concerned, and committed attitudes helped in erasing negative thoughts and building positive actions to ensure continuous progress in all areas.

My support systems were diversified. They included family members, teachers, friends, and other supporters with skills in mentoring. Their support ranged from verbal to nonverbal and from giving or seeking sources of reinforcement for me. These, I believe, will help others achieve similar benefits.

My gratitude is expressed to countless people who fertilized my plans to utilize the wealth of information from persons who willingly shared the good news of their success stories. In spite of challenges they encountered on their life journeys, they visualized success and overcame obstacles to experience wholeness of mind, body, and soul. For their collaboration in providing messages of faith, hope, and love, I give thanks.

Deep indebtedness is expressed to my family members for providing encouragement along the way. Their positive attitudes empowered me to continue to sacrifice time to write and share my thoughts.

My thankfulness is expressed to my publisher for numerous acts of kindness and expertise in making this book become a reality. The dedicated team at Providence House Publishers are tops on my priority list in the caring, concerned, and dedicated quality time spent in making this publication possible.

I am grateful to my colleague Mrs. Frances F. Shimotsu for additional help and positive thoughts in assisting me in the development of this manuscript. Her willingness to share her knowledge, skills, and creative approach helped this book become a reality.

For everyone else who shared or gave positive thoughts and recommendations, I express my sincere gratitude. May all of you be blessed immensely.

Part 1

Quality of experiences

compensates for limited time

utilized in the development of

personal growth activities.

Chapter One

INTRODUCTION

 Visions of success are seeds that come from ideas, images, desire, dedication, commitment, and communication in a structure that can provide crystallized plans of action.

Reflecting on the family roots of many people, I recognize persons who defied the odds and overcame adversities—not only to experience success, but also to help others achieve in various ways. A decision to share their stories began. In my perception, they are tools that build motivation within hearts, minds, and souls of readers.

As a traveler to all continents on study tours and for recreational purposes, I have encountered prosperous people in various careers whom I observed and interviewed to determine avenues of their success. Regardless of their social and cultural background, or the area of the world in which they lived, they attributed their upward mobility to strong support systems that elevated their self-esteem and convinced them that they could achieve their fondest dreams.

THIS BOOK PRESENTS A MULTICULTURAL/ MULTIETHNIC BACKGROUND OF PERSONS WHO HAVE SUCCEEDED IN MANY AREAS OF LIFE.

Realizing that opportunities for achievement are within everyone's reach regardless of race, creed, or color, this book presents a multicultural/multiethnic background of persons who have succeeded in many areas of life. They are passing the torch of success to activate a spiraling stream of hope, faith, and love to others on a global basis.

Life stories shared in this book have several commonalities, in that each person rose above handicapping conditions such as low economic status, limited opportunities to succeed, and social barriers. Yet they turned their adversities into opportunities to accomplish desired goals through support systems of dedicated mentors who either had competencies to provide necessary help, or could recruit those who would meet the needs that were identified.

Compensation of support offset what might have been failure had it not been for undaunted faith, expressed hope for a bright future, and unconditional love for those who overcame odds to succeed.

In each respondent's life, there was a desire to succeed and a willingness to find needs and fill them. This attracted rescuers and pathfinders to provide assistance and coping skills to overcome shackles of deprivation that otherwise would have hindered progress in development of maximum potential.

Data collection from observation, interviews, and written documents helped to answer these six questions:

1. What guideposts contributed to his/her success?
2. Who were the major players that provided support systems in planning, implementing, and monitoring their achievements?
3. Why did he/she choose his/her career path?
4. When did he/she decide that this was a vision that could be achieved?
5. Where is he/she currently at in life?
6. How is he/she passing the torch of success to others?

Based upon the confidentiality of contributors, in some cases the journey to success will omit the actual names of those whose stories are shared. The main ideas recorded will, hopefully, be beacons of light that will illuminate positive attitudes to stimulate an "I can do it, too" attitude for every reader.

Chapter Two

CASE STUDIES

SUZANNA

Born in the deep South in a rural agri-cultural setting, Suzanna encountered handicaps of sub-poverty conditions, a broken home, and limited human and material resources that would ensure success. Yet the tender, loving care of a maternal grandmother encouraged her with positive reinforcement to do her best in every activity she assumed.

Unable to read and write, the grandmother shared an abundance of faith and hope for Suzanna's success in making her world a better place with unconditional love for all people—even those who were frustrations to her spirit. The mother wit of the grandmother enabled her to share gems of wisdom in spite of her illiteracy. Some of her favorite affirmations shared with Suzanna were:

"Keep trying and you will succeed."

"God helps those who help themselves."

"Obey the Ten Commandments and you will succeed."

"Share, care, and love others for success."

"Give the world your best and the best will come back to you."

"Don't quit, because winners don't quit and quitters never win."

"Look your best, act your best, and be your best."

"Love, faith, and hope will help you cope in life's challenges."

"If at first you don't succeed, try again."

"If God is for you, no one can be against you."

"Believe in the power that protects you and you will achieve."

As Suzanna's role model, her grandmother mentored her and found people who could assist in obtaining a comprehensive education for her in home, school, and community. Seeds of self-confidence and self-respect were planted and bore fruits of success as Suzanna learned how to cope with things that were difficult, such as racism and inadequate finances to provide basic needs.

When she reached the fourth grade, her grandmother stated that, "Now, you can teach me to read." This was the realization that she could succeed in teaching her grandmother to learn to read the Bible; that task affirmed that Suzanna was a teacher.

This vision propelled her into taking steps to become a high self-esteemer that resulted in becoming a teacher after encountering many storms in life that were overcome through hard work, faith, hope, and unconditional love.

The African proverb, "It takes a whole village to educate a child," was tested and found to be true in Suzanna's life. Her grandmother enlisted the cooperation of the church, neighbors, teachers, and family members who helped her get off to a good start.

As the major player in Suzanna's development, her grandmother coordinated and collaborated in identifying needs

SEEDS OF SELF-CONFIDENCE AND SELF-RESPECT WERE PLANTED AND BORE FRUITS OF SUCCESS AS SUZANNA LEARNED HOW TO COPE WITH THINGS THAT WERE DIFFICULT, SUCH AS RACISM AND INADEQUATE FINANCES TO PROVIDE BASIC NEEDS.

and meeting them with appropriate assistance, which enabled Suzanna to develop a belief system and participate in the search for necessary help in curricular and extra-curricular activities.

The seeds for the idea of choosing teaching as her career path were sown early in childhood through continuous encouragement from her grandmother. Suzanna recalled that during her preschool years and later, when children would come to play, the grandmother would interact with them by encouraging them to play school on what they had learned in their Sunday School activities. She instilled leadership into Suzanna by saying, "Why don't you play the role of the teacher?" Smiles of satisfaction and the nodding of her head to indicate positive reaction could be evidenced from the grandmother as she sat in her rickety rocking chair on the porch during spring and summer months and in the old fashioned kitchen when the weather was too cold to play outside.

Before volunteerism was popular in Suzanna's one-room elementary school, her grandmother made weekly visits to the school to inquire about Suzanna's progress. The grandmother always reminded the teacher that she did not know how to read and write, but she could find help as needed from family and friends. She would continue communicating with the teacher to ask what help was needed, because Suzanna was going to be a teacher. She reinforced the conversation by saying: "With your help in school and the help I can get from others, she is going to be a great teacher like you." Smiling politely, the teacher assured the grandmother that Suzanna's progress was satisfactory. She assured her that if additional help was needed, she would be informed.

In spite of the inadequacy of equipment and teaching materials in this one-room educational facility, Suzanna was given extra assistance in the cultivation of her "inner-winning" spirit that was a follow-through of her goals. Spin-off benefits of the support of this caring, concerned, and committed grandmother, the positive attitudes of the teacher, and outside support from community and family helpers assisted Suzanna in becoming an honor roll student.

SUZANNA WAS GIVEN EXTRA ASSISTANCE IN THE CULTIVATION OF HER "INNER-WINNING" SPIRIT THAT WAS A FOLLOW-THROUGH OF HER GOALS.

Her first countywide educational recognition came when she was in the fourth grade and she won the spelling bee that was held in the auditorium of the junior high school for African-American students.

When Suzanna told her grandmother that she would be representing her school in the spelling bee, the grandmother was elated. She made herself a "committee of one" and went around telling her good news to everyone in her church and wherever she found listeners.

The day of the event, the grandmother made arrangements for a neighbor to drive her and Suzanna to the site where the spelling bee would take place. The two of them were dressed in their best Sunday clothes. The grandmother added her Argo–starched apron over her gingham dress, which was her trade mark for looking special whenever she was involved in any kind of educational activity. This included daily feedback from Suzanna about what she learned in school each day: the grandmother would put on a clean starched and ironed apron, take her favorite seat in the old rickety chair, and listen to every word Suzanna had to say. The grandmother would ask for a demonstration by saying, "Show me how your teacher taught you today!"

Practicing teaching behaviors gave Suzanna the desire and determination to become a certified teacher and to pursue teaching as a lifelong career.

After winning the spelling bee in competition with representatives from students on a countywide basis, the grandmother said: "Now, my child, it is time for you to continue to teach me how to read and write since you have learned so much from your school." She selected the family Bible as her textbook. After months of daily instruction, the grandmother became an avid reader. Her thirst for knowledge was revealed in many hours of study that extended beyond her structured home schooling.

Practicing teaching behaviors that were learned in school enhanced Suzanna's desire to become a certified teacher. The vision became an obsession and remained with her throughout her various stages of education from elementary school through college.

She succeeded in becoming an elementary school teacher. The desire to become a lifelong learner whetted her drive to earn several postgraduate degrees and positions as an educational supervisor and an administrator in early childhood education.

At this point in her life, Suzanna has spread knowledge, skills, and creativity globally and has remained committed to her love for her career. In spite of her success, she encountered many obstacles in life. The death of her grandmother before she entered college, her poverty-stricken environment with limited fiscal and human resources, and several negative thinkers placed extra burdens that hampered her progress.

Yet these adversities did not deter the goals and objectives that Suzanna had cherished from the support of her positive thinking and acting grand-mother. Whenever there were low points in her life, Suzanna would feast on gems of wisdom from her memory bank of affir-mations that she recalled hearing daily from her grandmother such as: "Where there is a will, there is a way," "You can make it if you try," "Believe in

WHENEVER THERE WERE LOW POINTS IN HER LIFE, SUZANNA WOULD FEAST ON GEMS OF WISDOM FROM HER MEMORY BANK OF AFFIRMATIONS THAT SHE RECALLED HEARING DAILY FROM HER GRANDMOTHER.

the power of God and you can overcome any problem," and others.

In spite of those who enjoyed criticizing her efforts to overcome poverty and who pointed out her deficiencies, Suzanna utilized the actions of doubters to increase opportunities to engage in positive imaging of what she was determined to achieve.

While Suzanna's grandmother was a positive force in her life, there were some counterattacks. For example, a hostile uncle, (her grandmother's youngest son), was a teenager when Suzanna was a preschooler. He had the job of baby-sitting her when the grandmother had to do domestic work. When she was older, he would have to walk her to and from school when the grandmother was not available. He detested these tasks and felt that his mother was giving her grandchild preferential treatment over him. Behind his mother's back, he criticized Suzanna and demeaned her in several ways, such as calling her "ugly," saying that her hair looked as awful as a "cockle-burr patch," and implying that she lived with them because her mother didn't want her. These negative statements made her cry; but the uncle threatened to do bodily harm if she told her grandmother. So she kept these negative statements a secret.

Being stimulated to succeed with an early support system, Suzanna's motivation to teach has been passed on to generations with positive rein-forcement. She has convinced others from diversified backgrounds and multicultural/multiethnic representations that everyone can learn and achieve their fondest dreams if they put forth every conceivable effort and reach out to support systems of mentors who are willing to share, care, and guide them from forests of despair to avenues of hope.

Summary

Suzanna's success was the result of a caring, concerned, and committed grandmother who found several people to supplement the training she received in school, church, and community organizations. They were local volunteers that ranged from teenagers to retired volunteers who tutored and guided Suzanna through mastery of curricular and extra-curricular activities that embarked and implemented education and service projects to meet the needs of younger children and the elderly.

She excelled in public speaking and enjoyed a career of teaching and administering educational programs. Presently, she is retired from her first career but has organized a consulting firm where she teaches others the lessons she learned through the years.

BARON

An inner-winner from early years, Baron also had difficulties in life as a victim of social ills in his community that put brakes on his progress. He lacked a strong parental supportive system and had inadequate tender, loving care, but an extended family of neighbors and church members filled the gaps of unconditional love that helped him become an effective husband and father of five children.

HE WAS TAUGHT BY HIS MATERNAL GRANDMOTHER . . . THAT HE COULD BECOME SUCCESSFUL IF HE PUT FORTH HIS BEST EFFORTS TO WORK HARD AND KEEP FAITH IN HIMSELF AS A CHOSEN PERSON OF HIS CREATOR.

He was taught by his maternal grandmother and devoted caretaking neighbors who stressed that he could become successful if he put forth his best efforts to work hard and keep faith in himself as a chosen person of his Creator. They helped him affirm that where there is a will, there is a way to overcome the tribulations that contributed to his low self-esteem.

Feelings of deficiencies in Baron's life were overcome by positive reinforcement given him by church members who helped his grandmother provide religious activities and opportunities to interact with caring and concerned peers in community events. Slowly his self-worth improved, and he began to make progress in school activities.

Completing high school and working at several after-school jobs enabled Baron to purchase necessities for himself and his grand-mother. Having an opportunity to buy clothes for himself, instead of wearing over-sized hand-me-downs, illuminated his personality.

Continuing to study after work, he realized his dream to become a postman. Later, he married and became a father of five children; life's chances for success improved. He was overjoyed with his ability to support a family and to buy a house for their comfort.

Years later, crippling arthritis forced Baron to take medical retirement from the post office.

Summary

Baron's rise from a life of sub-poverty conditions and low self-esteem proved that being a visionary could lift one to heights of excellence. Willingness to work and faith in the power of positive thinking will elevate self and others to high rungs on the ladder of success.

His ability to overcome challenges in life is proof that "whatever the mind can conceive and believe, it can achieve."

Determined to give back to others services that had been given to him as a youngster, Baron became a volunteer with his young children. Teachers, school administrators, and other parents noted his competence, dependability, and trustworthiness. He was elected as a Parent Involvement/Education Leader. This volunteer position provided opportunities for him to serve as a consultant to train parents to become effective partners in education.

> "WHATEVER THE MIND CAN CONCEIVE AND BELIEVE, IT CAN ACHIEVE."

His reputation gave him opportunities to travel with officials in several programs to participate in orientation and training programs in Parent Education/Involvement.

Continuing his education, he became a photographer and journalist in local weekly newspapers.

In addition to his career, he continued his work as a volunteer in schools, nursing homes, and church activities.

His exemplary contributions as a community helper have been recognized by several civic and educational activities. His outstanding services as a public speaker have given hope to many people to improve conditions in home, school, and community.

His faith in his Supreme Being, his hope for a better world for all people, and his unconditional love for all human beings have made Baron forget his problems by concentrating on solving the problems of others.

Consequently, his health conditions improved and the crippling effects of his arthritic conditions disappeared. He attributed this miracle to his belief that "it is more blessed to give than to receive." All who know him have noted his pleasing personality, his willingness to help others, and his determination to help others achieve.

His cup of love runs over with daily testimonials of the importance of giving of oneself to meet the needs of others. He states that he chose his life's work from early adulthood because it was the human thing to do and because it is a vital part of his religious beliefs in the Golden Rule of helping others realize their human potential.

THE RAYMOND FAMILY

Among my many friends are parents I have interacted with since the early fifties. It was during those beginning years of teaching when I encountered members of the Raymond family. The mother, a devoted parent and classroom volunteer, assisted school personnel in numerous ways. A resident of public housing with seven children, the mother was always involved in church, school, and community activities that provided a comprehensive program of teaching and learning activities for her children.

Having had the privilege to observe the growth and development throughout the successful completion of their public and higher education, it made faculty and staff rejoice to receive announcements from time to time of the Raymond children earning advanced degrees.

Recently, it was a thrilling experience for me to receive an invitation from the youngest child to attend her graduation from a school of law at a prestigious university.

WHEN ONE'S HEART, MIND, AND SOUL ARE FOCUSED ON HELPING OTHERS, ACHIEVEMENT WILL SOAR LIKE AN EAGLE.

Not only did Mrs. Raymond provide tender, loving care for her biological children, she assumed the mother role for many children who needed unconditional love to give them a feeling of belonging. As a role model for many neglected youngsters, Mrs. Raymond made her home a welcome haven of peace and happiness.

Her helping hands of faith, hope, and love are being replicated by not only members of her family, but by many lives she touched in the community with numerous acts of kindness—they are passing on good deeds to the less fortunate.

Summary

The success of the Raymond family serves as a beacon of light for overcoming obstacles. Mrs. Raymond illustrates that when one's heart, mind, and soul are focused on helping others, achievement will soar like an eagle. Helping "self" will crystallize faith, hope, and love into positive action for making the world a place of peace, harmony, and fulfillment. Her hard work achieved goals and objectives in the enhancement of excellence in all areas of life.

TONYA

Attending the International Conference on Self-Esteem held in Moscow, it was my pleasure to participate in the sessions that were coordinated by Tonya and her coworkers. It was my good fortune to be selected for home stay with and her family. The following year, I was able to reciprocate her hospitality when she came to the United States to participate in a workshop at Johns Hopkins University in Baltimore, Maryland, and she came to Richmond, Virginia, to visit my daughter and me.

Our cemented friendship of trust and unconditional love helped us to share information about our upbringing, career interests, and achievements, along with obstacles we had encountered along the way. While she was visiting with me, she shared the story of her background, which I later used in my column on self-esteem in the *Good News Herald*.

After her mother's death at an early age, Tonya was put into foster care where her self-esteem sank lower and lower with so many unpleasant situations. She was fortunate enough to meet caring, concerned, and committed teachers who elevated her self-esteem and helped her to attend college and graduate school. Majoring in psychology helped her study the function of the mind and behavior, which led her to utilize her maximum potential for success.

Now, as the mother of one child, she has helped her daughter to see herself as a positive human being with possibilities to achieve her fondest goals.

IF YOU CAN VISUALIZE HAPPINESS AND ACHIEVEMENT IN LIFE, YOUR FONDEST DREAMS WILL BE REALIZED.

She is operating a "Center for Children's Inventiveness" where she focuses on the creativity within each student in all areas of life.

She was given a grant to study at Johns Hopkins University in a Leadership Seminar, which enhanced her competencies and her creative skills to help those in need of other services.

Evidence of her capabilities were recognized as she assumed the major responsibility for organizing and implementing an International Conference on Self-Esteem with interpreters to help non-English speaking participants.

Summary

Tonya's success story is evidence that if you can visualize happiness and achievement in life, your fondest dreams will be realized, even if it means traveling from one continent to another to build a foundation of success.

She makes the old adage a reality that "If at first you don't succeed, try, try again."

 ## JULIA

Honor and praise are deserved by an outstanding mother, a super-excellent teacher, and an exemplary community worker whose achievements have enhanced excellence in education. This deserving citizen is Julia. As a former coworker, it was a privilege for me to observe her dedication and desire to excel with an interest in improving the teaching-learning process. Her creative approaches in bringing out the best in all students were evidenced in those who ranged from reluctant learners to gifted and talented.

Beginning as a school volunteer, she worked tirelessly to bring out the best in students. Later, she was employed as a paraprofessional and worked in supportive roles. In this capacity, she made weekly visits to parents 50 percent of her time and taught each one with a personalized home-learning activity, so that the parent could replicate the desirable teaching behavior with the child (or children) that had been developed cooperatively with the classroom teacher.

The love for teaching had mushroomed so strongly that it impelled Julia to enroll in college as an elementary education major on a part-time basis while continuing her employment as a teacher's assistant.

When she graduated, she was hired as a certified classroom teacher where she continues to demonstrate excellence in home, school, and community activities. She recruits, trains, and counsels parents and community volunteers to work with her children in the classroom and to provide community services that will improve living conditions in the community.

Her schedule is devoted to long hours of working with families, empowering them to excel, while providing adequate time for her biological children to develop their maximum potential.

Results of Julia's hard work, along with her volunteers, show that each year her students excel in academic and extra-curricular activities. They are recipients of awards in creative activities as the Young Authors Book Club, poetry, and drama, and their grade point averages are in the top level for the school.

EXCELLENCE . . . WILL BE REALIZED WHEN ONE IS CARING, CONCERNED, AND COMMITTED TO MAKING THE WORLD A BETTER PLACE, AND WHEN ONE BRINGS OUT THE *BEST* IN SELF AND OTHERS.

Summary

Julia demonstrated that excellence in achievement of desires and dreams will be realized when one is caring, concerned, and committed to making the world a better place, and when one brings out the *best* in self and others.

Overcoming challenges in her life and in the lives of others illustrates that with faith, hope, and unconditional love, all things are possible.

Replication of Julia's training helped volunteers and others increase their competencies.

MARTIN

Unaware that his marriage had gone sour, Martin came home and found a note from his wife saying that she was leaving him and their three children, ages five, three, and one, for him to raise, because she was tired of family life.

This traumatic experience, according to Martin, was overwhelming. He had to resign from his job as a truck driver because of a nervous condition he encountered after his wife left him with the young children. His small savings dwindled and he lost his mortgaged house and had to get an apartment in a public housing development because his only income was unemployment compensation.

His road to recovery was filled with bitterness and helplessness. With swallowed pride, he became a welfare recipient, which enabled him to take care of his children.

With no close relatives, he discovered the value of friendship when neighbors assisted him with baby-sitting when he had to be away from home to take care of business. Having lost his car from lack of funds to make payments on it, Martin had to depend on public transportation or a free ride from a neighbor.

Finally, he enrolled his five-year-old in kindergarten and the three-year-old was accepted into a federally-funded preschool program. He and the one-year-old visited child development centers. Whenever he could get a baby sitter, he would spend time as a school volunteer.

This experience helped him to discover his love for helping children grow and develop. Prior to the unfortunate break up of his home, Martin had resorted to earning money for his family and his wife had done most of the home activities with the children.

Little by little, his hatred for his wife's actions turned to forgiveness. He began accepting the blame for her desertion. He thought that this young woman had become a victim of burnout and neglect because he had worked all of the time and taken overtime whenever he had the opportunity. His focus was on making money while neglecting to give personal attention to his wife and children.

His health improved and he found part-time work in a child-care center. This enabled him to be home in the evenings with his children and to provide small compensation to a neighbor who kept his one-year-old while he was at work.

School personnel advised Martin to apply for a grant to help him go to a community college to prepare himself for a career in early childhood education, since he had expressed a desire to learn more about how to guide the growth and development of children. He did and became an honor student and participated in several school-related activities. At the end of two years, he had completed the requirements for graduating from the community college. According to him, his thirst for knowledge had elevated. He transferred to a four-year college and maintained his honor role status on a scholarship grant.

Upon graduation, he was employed as a teacher in the elementary school where his children attended. He stated that this was a joyful event, but there was a void in his life. His guilty conscience elevated his desire to find his wife and express his sorrow for having neglected her and their children. While concentrating on making money to take care of physical needs, he had neglected the emotional, social, and intellectual needs of his family.

Through some research, he located his wife in another state, where she was employed as a postal worker and lived alone in an apartment. Interaction started when she confessed that she had regretted leaving her family, but pride had kept her from returning home.

After about six months of communication and occasional weekend visits, love for each other grew, and the children were ecstatic that they had both a father and mother to love them. They were reunited as a family.

> THE CHILDREN WERE ECSTATIC THAT THEY HAD BOTH A FATHER AND MOTHER TO LOVE THEM. THEY WERE REUNITED AS A FAMILY.

Martin enrolled in graduate school and became a counselor. His wife entered undergraduate school in the department of social work. Now both are volunteers in marriage counseling services.

They enjoy helping families see the importance of spending quality time together. Their positive interactions demonstrated that happiness, good health, and unity of purpose will result from living productive lives with children.

Summary

Martin's achievement is exemplary. His uniqueness is visible in his ability to forgive and to avoid passing blame to his adversities.

His dedication to overcoming obstacles and turning them to opportunities for success is commendable.

 JACKIE

Growing up in rural West Virginia, Jackie enjoyed walking barefooted. After getting a divorce from her husband, she migrated to Virginia to live with relatives. When she brought her two children, ages seven and nine, to be enrolled in school, she came barefooted with her long blonde hair rolled up in curlers.

The school was all white until the law was passed for integrated schools. Some unrest occurred and private schools were popping up in many places including basements of churches and abandoned buildings. Some were substandard. Enrollment in other excellent private schools escalated. "For Sale" signs were going up where "white flight" left the city and moved to counties where all white people lived to avoid integration.

In order to solve the problem, the Federal Government provided grants to provide retreats and resources that would promote the healthy interaction of diversified groups of parents and school personnel.

Trained personnel were hired to facilitate "togetherness" with unity of purpose in enhancing excellence in the teaching-learning process of improved race relations.

Schools that had previously been all black or all white were paired, and weekend retreats were held to increase understanding and appreciation of diversity in the schools.

Jackie signed up to go on the first retreat that included the school's faculty and parents along with the same proportion of faculty and parents from a previously all black school. She did not know until the buses arrived from each school and room assignments had been made that the retreat site would house two people to each room: her roommate would be a black woman. Jackie refused to stay in her room. She said she had never lived near any black person and she did not intend to start. She wanted to know whether the bus driver could take her home because the retreat site was at least twenty-five miles off a beaten path, and she did not know her way home if she decided to hitchhike.

She was told that all rooms were filled and all assignments made with a black and white person sharing the same room. She said, "Well I'll just sit up and sleep in a chair the whole weekend because I'll not go in that room."

After the evening meal, all workshop and recreational activities people retired to their assigned rooms. True to her word, Jackie sat in a chair to sleep. The facilitator talked to her to find out why she did not want to sleep in the room with a black woman. Jackie said she did not trust her roommate, she didn't like her, and she had never slept in a room nor had anything to do with black people. After leaving her for about an hour, the facilitator returned and told her she looked uncomfortable and pleaded with her to go and get in her bed to rest. Again she refused.

Finally, the facilitator asked her if there was any black woman at the retreat that Jackie would trust to share the room for two nights (Friday and

Saturday) at the retreat. After thinking about the question, she said she would reluctantly share the room with the educational supervisor whom she had interacted with in some school activities.

Friendship began when the room assignment was made, and lasted for many years. Both women talked about the families, hobbies, and things that made them happy.

When the retreat was over on Sunday, they exchanged telephone numbers and began to communicate whenever they felt the desire to talk together, reflecting on what had been learned on the retreat. The most rewarding conversation, according to Jackie, was when she said, "Now, I think I like black people."

THE MOST REWARDING CONVERSATION, ACCORDING TO JACKIE, WAS WHEN SHE SAID, "NOW, I THINK I LIKE BLACK PEOPLE."

After being encouraged to go to school to get her GED, Jackie did just that. Then she enrolled in college with a grant that the federally funded program provided. She was an honor student and became a teacher.

Four years later, she wrote a letter to the program director stating that in addition to teaching, she was enrolled in a graduate school of education and would like for the director to speak to her university class about the program that changed her life from negative to positive and made her life worth living. Accepting the invitation, a date and time were scheduled. When the director arrived, there was a smiling young lady waiting at the elevator who said: "I am so glad to see you. I will be introducing you to our class." It was not until she spoke that the director recognized who Jackie was. She had a complete makeover with sophisticated mannerisms, charisma, and self-assurance. Informing the guest speaker that she expected to be awarded a master's degree in four months, Jackie said that she had bought a house, both of her children were doing well in school, and she was enjoying teaching. Just before they entered the classroom, Jackie asked: "Aren't you happy that I am an example of one whose behavior was modified?"

NO MATTER WHERE ONE COMES FROM OR HOW LIMITED ONE'S PERCEPTION IS, BEHAVIOR CAN BE MODIFIED AND THE MIND CAN BE CONVERTED FROM NEGATIVE TO POSITIVE.

Her introduction of the director and her story about the experience at the retreat brought tears of joy to many eyes. Jackie stated that she is spending a lot of time volunteering and sharing ways to improve race relations.

Giving back to the needy what had been given to her—the opportunity to succeed and to demonstrate that diversity—is important in making the world a better place. This testimony convinced many listeners that our challenge is to keep touching lives in positive ways.

Summary

Jackie convinces readers that no matter where one comes from or how limited one's perception is, behavior can be modified and the mind can be converted from negative to positive. She demonstrates that if one is willing to listen and become open to possibilities, all things are possible.

WILLIAM AND DAVID

In the early seventies after the integration of schools in Richmond, Virginia, William (black) and David (white) were attending the same kindergarten class. These five-year-olds had similar interests in building blocks, painting, jungle gyms, puzzles, and enjoyed working together whenever teamwork was required.

David was going to be six years old two months before William. His parents lived in suburbia in an upper-middle-class neighborhood, while William and his mother lived in the inner city in a low-income neighborhood.

In preparation for David's birthday, his mother asked him to name the friends he wanted to invite to his home for his party. He stated that he only wanted to invite his *best friend*, William, to come and spend the weekend with him so they could have a long time to play together. His mother thought that would be a good idea. Since she did not know William, she decided to go to his classroom and to take a note of invitation to send to his mother, asking permission for him to come for the weekend to help David celebrate his birthday.

When she visited the classroom and shared her plan for David's birthday celebration, the teacher asked, "Are you certain you are going to invite William to spend the weekend at your house?" The mother replied, "Yes."

The teacher asked her if she would like to meet William. Again, the answer was "Yes." It was lunchtime, and the mother noticed that her son was sitting next to a black child. When she moved to the table David hopped up and said, "Hi Mom, this is my friend William. He said he will come to my house for my birthday!"

According to the mother, she was shocked. Not once did it enter her mind that William was black.

She said she put the note in her purse and said, "We'll talk about it when you come home."

Feeling worried, she stated that she did not know how she could tell her son that inviting this child to spend the weekend would not please her nor her neighbors.

After dinner that evening, she explained to David that William lived too far away, so he should invite one of his friends that lived in their neighborhood. She said David was adamant: "I want William to stay because he is my *best* friend!"

That night after David had gone to bed, she explained the situation to her husband and said she didn't think it was wise to invite William to spend the weekend because of fear of what the neighbors would say. Some of them had put their children in private school and others were reluctant about school integration because they feared that blacks would soon want to integrate the neighborhood.

Her husband said, "I think we should honor his request and invite William. After all, he is our first child and we must instill in him that all people are the same."

The next day, she sent the note home to William's mother and asked her to reply by writing or calling her. Several days passed and no reply came. She decided to go to school and ask William what his mother had said. He reported that she had said: "I'll think about it."

She asked him if he knew his telephone number. He did and gave it to her. When she called the mother and asked her to give William permission to visit for the birthday celebration, William's mother replied, "I don't think this is a good idea. I don't allow my child to stay with strangers."

David's mother said that she could understand how she felt. Then she asked William's mother to give her permission to visit her, since their sons were such good friends at school. Permission was granted.

When she went to visit, she took David with her. While the mothers were talking, the boys were romping and playing nonstop. The request for William to spend the weekend was repeated and the mother was invited to come, too. She declined.

The next request was for both families to come together for a visit to eat lunch and she could see where David's parents lived. William's mother stated that she did not have a car and she was a widow who worked everyday to make ends meet for their survival. After further discussion, she agreed to come because David's mother volunteered to pick her up after working hours.

The visit was cordial. Both boys obviously enjoyed playing together. David assumed the role of host and asked William's mother to please let William come to celebrate his birthday on the appointed weekend. She said, "Since you insist, he may come." The reluctance in her voice was clearly evident according to the interpretation of David's mother.

When the date for the weekend visit came, David's mother stated that when she went to pick William up, he came out the door immaculately dressed with a silver dollar in his hand. He handed it to David and said, "My mother said this is your birthday present."

Years passed and the boys remained friends. They went to the same high school. Both graduated with honors, received scholarships, and attended the same college. Both decided to go to law school. With the help of grants and student loans, they finished with honors.

After marriage to classmates, they practiced law in different cities but still maintained contact and both shared how they demonstrated brotherly love.

According to David's mother, both families visit each other and affirmed that the children made integration a reality. Their demonstration of acceptance of each other as human beings, regardless of difference in race, proved that racism is a learned behavior.

THEIR DEMONSTRATION OF ACCEPTANCE OF EACH OTHER AS HUMAN BEINGS, REGARDLESS OF DIFFERENCE IN RACE, PROVED THAT RACISM IS A LEARNED BEHAVIOR.

As role models of success, they are still enhancing peaceful relationships that can be emulated at home, school, and the work-place.

Summary

The quotation "A little child shall lead them" is verified in the positive actions of these young boys. Their unconditional love and support for each other caused their parents to become followers of their offspring: true leaders for making unity in our multicultural/multiethnic society a reality.

NATHAN

Nathan was born in the cotton belt of a rural section of the deep South, where he and his family had not traveled over ten miles from his birthplace. Nathan dreamed of what life was like in other places. From time to time, visitors came to his little country church, and he heard of their successes in other parts of the country.

Whenever he had a chance to speak to a visitor, he would ask about their cotton, corn, and soybean crops, and how much they could earn from each crop. When they told him that there were no farms in the northern cities where they lived and that people earned a living in other careers as factory workers, producers of goods and services, and as trained professionals, this information whetted Nathan's desire to relocate to a place that sounded heavenly to him.

His main job on the farm was to plow the land with a mule, planting seeds, chopping wood for cooking and heating, picking cotton, raising chickens and cows, gardening, and other menial tasks on the farm where he and his family had been sharecroppers for many years. They lived in a three-room wooden shack with no running water or indoor toilets.

After working hours, the sweltering heat of the summer was cooled with hand fans given by funeral directors to the church attendees. In winter, the only warmth Nathan's family received was from the one fireplace and the wood-burning stove where the food was cooked.

Nathan attended a one-room school about four months each year. He had many absences because he was required to do farm work or because he did not have adequate clothing to wear. He repeated grades several times because he could not achieve minimum competencies. This did not bother Nathan because that was the way of life in the rural delta area.

Life changed for Nathan and his family when his aunt, uncle, and cousins came to visit them from Chicago. They convinced the family to let eleven-year-old Nathan come to live with them in order for him to have an opportunity to go to school everyday and to prepare himself for a career that would empower him to make a living for himself, and to give him an opportunity to interact with their four children whose ages ranged from nine to fourteen years old.

Listening to the children tell about their schools and activities they were involved in like scouting, music lessons, YMCA sports, and others, Nathan was excited and wanted to experience these opportunities.

After much coaxing from the aunt and uncle— along with a promise that they would bring Nathan home for a visit in six months and that he could decide then if he wanted to stay on the farm—Nathan's parents finally agreed.

With teary eyes, Nathan's mother packed all of his clothing in a pillowcase because they did not own any luggage. Both Nathan and his father shed a few tears when they said good-bye.

Getting into his aunt and uncle's late-modeled car, Nathan's eyes were glued to the back window as he kept waving to his parents, who were also waving to him.

Riding in a car many miles was a novel experience. He felt a little afraid, thinking that his uncle would run off the road or his car would get hit by an oncoming car. After talking a while, his cousins fell asleep; but Nathan felt too uncomfortable to sleep. He was happy to be leaving farm life for something better, but he was feeling lonely for his parents and the familiar surrounding of his shack.

During the trip, his uncle stopped for gasoline and for everyone to go to the bathroom. Nathan looked around for an outdoor toilet but he did not see one. His cousins told him to follow them to the restroom. This ordeal of flushing the toilet was new and strange to him.

Their next stop was at a restaurant where they went in for dinner. Seeing tables covered with cloths, a centerpiece with a flower, cloth napkins, and silver utensils, Nathan thought these were too pretty to eat on. In fact, the menus were full of things he wished his parents could see. He thought that they would not believe all of these strange things.

Ordering a meal was something he had never done, so he thought if he said he was not hungry he could avoid being embarrassed by not knowing how to order. After convincing him that his body needed a little food to last until they reached home, he decided that he would eat a chicken dinner with a glass of milk. That was familiar to him, and he enjoyed the meal.

Arriving at his new home in Chicago was an awesome experience. Seeing skyscrapers, buses, trains, and people rushing on streets made him think that the city was too busy for him.

His aunt, uncle, and cousins escorted him on a tour of their house of eight rooms with two bathrooms and a recreational center in the basement. This made Nathan feel that he would get lost and be unable to find his way around this house that seemed too big for people to live in.

Sharing a room with his eleven-year-old cousin made him feel better—he would not have to sleep in a room alone. They played with some games and watched television until his aunt said that it was bedtime and they had to put out the lights and go to sleep. Nathan, however, could not go to sleep because the city noises of trains, horns honking, and other sounds kept him awake for hours. He was ready to go home to a quieter place where dogs would bark, roosters would crow in early morning hours, and cows would moo every now and then.

THE POWER OF THE EXTENDED FAMILY AS A SUPPORT SYSTEM IS EVIDENCED IN THE OUTCOME OF THIS FAMILY'S TENDER, LOVING CARE THAT REACHED OUT TO LIFT AN INDIGENT FAMILY FROM CLOUDS OF DOUBT TO SUNLIGHT OF OPPORTUNITY.

Nathan's first day in his new school seemed like a disaster to him. His aunt took him to the office to register him after buying him new clothes. Since he did not have a health record, she had to take him to a doctor to get needed immunizations. He hated this ordeal. After filling out several forms, Nathan was placed in an ungraded classroom for personalized instruction. He was a good listener and worked hard to complete assignments. He went beyond expectations to excel in all of his courses. His teacher, principal, and supportive services staff reviewed Nathan's phenomenal progress and recommended that he be transferred to a middle school's seventh grade regular class.

This was done, and he became an honor roll student every semester.

Summary

The power of the extended family as a support system is evidenced in the outcome of this family's tender, loving care that reached out to lift an indigent family from clouds of doubt to sunlight of opportunity.

THE LEE FAMILY

Striving to earn a living with the minimum wages of a father, an invalid mother, and three school-age boys brought challenges that made one wonder how they could survive without public assistance. But the Lee family did.

The oldest boy convinced his father that he could be a newspaper salesman to help bring in additional income. Only ten years old, he encouraged his father to fill out the necessary papers for the job; he and his brothers decided they were going to be outstanding in the world of business.

The boys started out going from door to door to secure clients for their afternoon paper. Neighbors were kind and took subscriptions because they knew the economic challenges this family faced. The paper route started out with 30 families and increased to 125 families. This added to the family income.

Later when the teenager with the morning paper route left home to go to college, the boys had a family meeting with their parents and convinced them that they could take over that route before going to school.

Soon, with the father's assistance, the paper routes grew and the income helped the family to move out of their rented home into their first small home ownership. Neighbors helped them make repairs to make the house livable. Rejoicing was a part of their daily interaction with each other.

> AT WEEKLY FAMILY MEETINGS, THE FATHER SHARED GEMS OF WISDOM WITH THE BOYS, AND THE MOTHER HELPED THEM REMEMBER THE NEED TO HELP THE LESS FORTUNATE.

At weekly family meetings, the father shared gems of wisdom with the boys, and the mother helped them remember the need to help the less fortunate. Not only did they tithe to their church, but they also selected their favorite charity and shared a portion of their savings with it.

In addition, the father had the boys go with him to the local bank to start a small savings account that was increased slowly on a monthly basis.

Their business grew when they added the sales of candy, magazines, and other items. Throughout their years in elementary and secondary schools, they became known as the "Lee Business Family" and won community awards of "Citizens Most Likely to Succeed."

The instructions of the father and positive guidance of the invalid mother taught the boys "It is more blessed to give than to receive."

In addition to being salesmen, they worked hard in school, and all three received full scholarships to college. After college, where they had business-related majors, the young men opened a store selling groceries and a variety of merchandise. Then they expanded from one to three stores that were profitable.

Summary

The Lee family learned the value of living within one's means and sharing and caring for the less fortunate. Their lessons in life are evidence of "where there is a will, there is a way."

Part 2

YESTERDAY IS HISTORY,

TOMORROW IS A MYSTERY,

TODAY IS A GIFT,

THAT'S WHY IT IS CALLED THE PRESENT.

—ANONYMOUS

Chapter Three

Attributes of Strong Support Systems

 Based upon the characteristics of the support systems cited in these case studies, evidences of strengths were as follows:

PHYSICAL

Healthy bodies were part and parcel of the immediate and extended families in the study. Significant attitudes of "I will succeed" and "I can overcome" were present, making the journey of success an obtainable goal.

INTELLECTUAL

Capacities for setting and achieving predetermined objectives were present in support systems that utilized positive thoughts and actions in planning, implementing, and monitoring step-by-step activities with a focus of mental alertness.

HOME AND FAMILY INFLUENCE

Backgrounds of achievers in each support system had the support and positive reinforcement of a foundation of parents or (parenting ones) who operated on the premise that success was operating in the realm of possibility. They operated with open minds, believing that all things are possible for those who are willing to risk in order to overcome adversities in life.

> ALL THINGS ARE POSSIBLE FOR THOSE WHO ARE WILLING TO RISK IN ORDER TO OVERCOME ADVERSITIES IN LIFE.

ETHICAL VALUES

Right conduct and practices were involved in the professional standards that propelled close inspection of every action to determine its conformity with truth. All issues were examined to analyze the difference between acceptable and unacceptable behavior and to arrive at the correct solution to any problem.

SOCIAL AND CULTURAL AWARENESS

Operating in a diverse population of needs and interests in a multicultural/multiethnic society resulted in recognition of the varied strengths of support systems.

The enhanced growth and development of all stakeholders in the search for success, with positive thoughts and positive actions, was evidenced.

CAREER DEVELOPMENT

Professional growth was enhanced when mentorship programs were evidenced to assist those persons who were supported in decision-making and goal-setting activities. Rungs on the ladder of success were upward and onward in the mastery of various levels, as stages of success were realized.

The avenues of success were comprehensive in nature and involved physical, mental, emotional, social, and spiritual growth, as well as supportive services in an atmosphere of faith, hope, and unconditional love.

DESIRE, DREAMS, DARING, AND DETERMINATION

The human resources necessary for the success of effective support systems were those who wanted to see successful enterprises materialize as benefits to everyone in an organization of caring, concerned, and committed members. Dreamers were those with visions who perceived the possibility of ideas coming true when accompanied with positive actions. These were generated into a composite structure that involved the total

commitment for positive outcomes of all stake-
holders in the anticipated achievement of
imaginary goals.

Daring supporters of dreams were those coura-
geous enough to buy into the dreams and brave
enough to assume challenges to take part in risking
time, talents, and financial resources to make
dreams come true.

Determination sparkled with assumed power
from all participants expressing the willingness to
work for satisfactory outcomes that addressed and
met needs for successful conclusions.

The multiplication of perceived ingredients for
generating ideas and selling them to others mushroomed into a structure that made clouds of
uncertainties transform to sunlight of realities.
While the desire began with a single member of a
family discerning the presence of needs, it conta-
giously spread positive effects to a system of
supporters, who became contaminated with faith,
hope, and unconditional love for perceived ideas.

THE GARDEN OF LIFE INCLUDES
PEOPLE, PLACES, AND THINGS
THAT MAKE THE WORLD A
BLESSING OF BEAUTY FOR
COPING WITH CHALLENGES.

Chapter Four

REFLECTIONS ON RESEARCH RELATED TO THE EFFECTIVENESS OF SUPPORT SYSTEMS FOR SUCCESS

 In Frank J. Sparzo's research on *The ABC'S of Behavior Change*, he emphasized the importance of "selective reinforcement."[1] He affirmed: "To improve or increase a person's performance, positively reinforce its occurrence."[2] Several case studies were presented in his publication, documenting that his model, which consists of a nine-step process, is effective when the plan is practiced.

Research of over twenty years in duration in the parent Education Follow-Through program revealed that a support system of home, school, and community yielded positive results in terms of developing the "whole child" physically, mentally, socially, and emotionally. The program was nationally validated by the Joint Dissemination Panel composed of researchers from the National Institution of Education and the National Office of Education.

Sirgay Sanger and John Kelly's research illustrated how working mothers can be highly effective as parents by giving quality time and involving fathers and/or other caregivers with young children.[3] Data shared from these authors' Early Care Center in New York City reported on numerous success stories of the first four years of a child's life. The importance of a support team emphasized criteria for caregivers to be sensitive, loving, and warm companions for children. Respect for the caregiver is necessary for a mutual support system.

Important information was shared on the importance of nurturing all children in large families. More support should be given to needy children, suggests Dr. Katherine Schlaerth, pediatrician and family counselor.[4] On the other hand, gifted children should have special attention as needed to enhance their strengths and to keep them focused on achieving their maximum potential.

Loving Your Child Is Not Enough—Positive Discipline that Works by Nancy Samalin outlines the importance of reaching out to a support system for help in the process of child growth and development. She states, "If you use words that encourage others to cooperate with you instead of blaming them for their shortcomings you are more likely to elicit the response you desire. If you try this with a spouse, grandparent, teacher, caregiver, or anyone else who plays a significant role in your child's life, you may gain an ally who will give you valuable support."[5]

Samalin stresses the importance of positive communication skills that should start early in life, preparing children for later success. She adds that using empathic responses—even occasionally—will give children a new model for communicating with their peers, siblings, and teachers as well as with parents.[6]

Thomas and Eileen Paris provide a guide to conscious parenting in their publication *I'll Never Do to My Kid What My Parents Did to Me*.[7] As marriage and family counselors, as well as parents, this couple reports on their varied experiences and share pertinent information on the parenting process as an outline for flexible family relations. They contend that the health of the larger community depends on the emotional health of our families. This in turn affects the well-being of the adults and children that make up these families. They contend that "the problem for the community of nations is the same as that for individuals within a family." The Parises explain how to maintain independence and uniqueness while nourishing unity and connectedness among all people. They

USING EMPATHIC RESPONSES—EVEN OCCASIONALLY—WILL GIVE CHILDREN A NEW MODEL FOR COMMUNICATING WITH THEIR PEERS, SIBLINGS, AND TEACHERS AS WELL AS WITH PARENTS.

explain the importance of utilizing methods and procedures they believe to be best in helping their children develop maximum potential, rather than using patterns of parenting outlined in the past performances of their parents.[8]

In *Don't Be Afraid to Discipline,* Dr. Ruth Peters states: "Happiness, it seems, is the result of good parenting. You cannot buy it, fake it, talk your child into it or manipulate the world to provide it. Happiness is a state of comfort that develops when you are content with your relationship with others, having developed a healthy balance between fulfilling your own needs while helping others with theirs. It is the security of knowing that your child can control his emotions and behavior so that no matter what challenges he faces, he can act appropriately."[9]

In Stephen R. Covey's publication, *The 7 Habits of Highly Effective People,* he states that in the synergism of nature, everything is related to everything else. He declares that "the relationship of the parts is also the power in creating a synergistic culture inside a family or an organization. The more genuine the involvement, the more sincere and sustained the participation in analyzing and solving problems, the greater the release of everyone's creativity and of their commitments to what they create."[10]

Lawrence J. Greene shares *1001 Ways to Improve Your Child's School Work.* He reminds readers that there is a mutually shared objective between a child's teacher, parents, and school administration that is designed to help the child become skilled, productive, self-sufficient, and self-confident. He declares that the goal is attainable only when everyone is willing to work together.[11]

In discussing the importance of self-esteem and self-confidence, Greene suggests that these must be earned. In helping children become resilient, they can gain self-esteem by solving problems, providing many challenges, handling frustration, and dealing with setbacks. They earn it by working hard, persevering, and thinking strategically. As they develop their talents and experience their own power, they will acquire increasing self-sufficiency and self-appreciation. These qualities are the benchmark of good self-esteem, according to Greene.[12]

Stephanie Marston declares in her book *The Magic of Encouragement* that "parents need a supportive community, a network of people they can turn to for advice, support and to share ideas."[13] She added, "We weren't meant to raise our children in isolation. We need other parents with whom we can discuss our challenges as well as our joys."

Walter Barbe suggests in *Growing Up Learning* that parents should be cognizant of children's needs. When necessary, team members should be recruited to develop an educational plan to help children develop their maximum strength. He suggests that "modality-based education is one approach that is effective for many learners who have known little success in school. It is a tool for diagnosing problems and a plan for realizing achievement for gifted, average and slow learners."[14] Barbe emphasizes that learning is a process that grows as children mature and gain knowledge, skills, and creativity as they pass through various stages of development in living, acting, and reacting to experiences in their environment.

In *How to Influence Children*, Charles Schaefer explains the importance of bringing relatives closer to children through family reunions that will bring a child's heritage to the forefront. He states that "pride in the family history and ancestors should also be encouraged."[15] Research cited in this publication reveals that positive, respectful communication with each family member strengthens a support system. One of several guidelines that are effective in influencing children is a "Family Council Meeting." Schaefer states that "Family meetings help everyone in the family to learn to listen, to negotiate, and be concerned about the welfare of the entire group."[16]

. . . POSITIVE, RESPECTFUL COMMUNICATION WITH EACH FAMILY MEMBER STRENGTHENS A SUPPORT SYSTEM.

Theodore Isaac Rubin describes in *Child Potential* that the "cooperative or enabling household" is one in which there is outreach beyond the nuclear family to transcend generation gaps. He states: "This feeling for members of other generations and extended family gives even more of a sense of belonging and strength."[17] He contends that loving each other is most important in building a support system:

The cooperative household members demonstrate strong feelings, values, priorities and social
consciousness. They are flexible. They can hear
each other. They don't engage in contests. They
give of themselves and they can give without
feeling depleted. Without conscious awareness,
they know that love is not a fixed fund and then
used up. Loving generates more love. They love
each other and are enablers to each other.[18]

In paraphrasing statements made by Rubin, it is
evident that unity of purpose and unity of strength
are guidelines for developing the potential of every
child. The acquisition of knowledge of one individual
can be replicated in another to strengthen support
systems of growth and development. This idea is no
doubt the forerunner of education in groups in order
to pass the torch of understanding and building a
foundation of success in later learning.

Schaefer expounds on the importance of a
support system through the development of a *real
family* spirit. He suggests that concerted efforts
should be made to stress human relations within
the family with mutual acceptance, protection,
enjoyment, support, and consideration. He further
suggested that "pride in family history should be
encouraged to give children an ego boost to mini-
mize feelings of alienation and loneliness."[19]

He notes, "When a family spends time together in
common activities, a sense of cohesiveness
develops,"[20] such as doing things together to establish

family traditions, celebrations, and rituals. He suggests that discussion meetings and family projects will enhance a supportive team effort to establish effective communication and unconditional love for children to observe role models of excellence.

AN ORGANIZATION OF SUPPORT GROUPS FOR HELPING EACH OTHER WILL CRYSTALLIZE A CADRE OF SUPPORT AS NEEDED FROM TEAM PLAYERS.

Susan Crites Price and Tom Price indicate in their publication, *The Working Parents' Help Book* that "friends provide important emotional support and practical help for parents."[21] They suggest that an organization of support groups for helping each other will crystallize a cadre of support as needed from team players.

A fantastic support system is reported in James McBride's New York Times best seller, *The Color of Water: A Black Man's Tribute to His White Mother,* in which a strong matriarch with a dozen sons and daughters overcame poverty, the physical handicap of a lame leg, being widowed twice, and being a white woman living in an all black neighborhood.[22] With an inner-winning spirit, she propelled all twelve children to grow, develop, and earn success in higher education with diversified careers that included medical doctors, historians, a nurse, a journalist, a business person, a researcher, program administrators, and others.

The mother demonstrated numerous evidences of wanting only the best for her children. She sacrificed to send them to the best schools and instilled in them the idea that education would empower them to be "a somebody." When her mixed African-American children would question her about her color, she replied she was "light-skinned," and when they asked her about the color of God, she replied, "God is the color of water."

The success of this family resulted from the strong support system of a devoted mother with a positive mental attitude, excellent educations, and a few caring, concerned, and committed supporters.

I shared several guidelines for building a support system in my publication *Climbing the Success Ladder*.[23] I emphasized that the strength of a support system is depended upon each member of the team making concerted efforts to find needs and fill them. Suggested guidelines in planning, implementing, and evaluating a support system for continuous success in parent education performance are as follows:

- Identify a group of interested parents and form a community of supporters
- Share problems related to child rearing practices and how to cope with challenges related to child growth and development
- Find human resources for providing assistance in solving identified problems
- Organize subgroups to work on special phases of common problems
- Set regular meeting dates for sharing progress reports
- Read widely on topics of interest

- Recruit volunteer specialists to conduct workshops for parent groups related to identified problems
- Organize exchange clubs of books, toys, games, etc.
- Disseminate knowledge, skills, and techniques to a wider audience via newsletters, radio, and television talk shows.[24]

I also shared my Ten Commandments of Successful Parent Education Performance as follows:

1. Be a good role model and engage in two-way communication.
2. Have a positive and trusting attitude.
3. Discipline with love and respect.
4. Understand and meet the unique needs of every child.
5. Give sincere, honest praise lavishly.
6. Be patient and non-judgmental.
7. Have high expectations in a partnership of teaching and learning.
8. Share high quality time and learning resources with children.
9. Experience joy in achievements, and express humor in a relaxed atmosphere.
10. Create an environment of peace, beauty, and emotional well-being.[25]

The importance of strong support systems is not a novel idea. In 1847 Horace Mann reported on the duty of the old generation to the new in his essay titled "The Ground of the Free School System," published by the Massachusetts Board of Education in the *Tenth Annual Report*. Mann emphasized that the business of education is not the responsibility of one entity; it is a cooperative venture of all who possess a stake directly or indirectly in the survival of human beings on planet earth.[26]

In 1958 a special studies report funded by the Rockefeller Brothers' Fund reiterated the importance of teamwork in the pursuit of excellence in education. The fifth report of the study series titled *The Pursuit of Excellence in Education and the Future of America* advised that "society as a whole must come to the aid of the individual in helping to achieve excellence and still maintain individual uniqueness."[27]

Wholeness of mind, body, and soul results in the cultivation and growth of a strong support system. Helping individuals and groups to visualize success is an ongoing process for experiencing opportunities to analyze and crystallize thoughts for positive actions towards predetermined goals.

Stability in support systems enhances a structure for the development of belief models of behavior that will brighten the outlook of each member in a group to transform doubts to possibilities, pain to gain, and adversities to opportunities, to set and achieve realistic goals.

Reformation of "I can't" attitudes to "I can and I will" attitudes will be the end result of the transfer of vision to hope, hope to faith, and faith to unconditional love in powerful, positive systems.

Chapter Five

EXAMPLES OF EFFECTIVE STRONG SUPPORT SYSTEMS

THE BERKELEY FAMILY
A Family Reunion

Migrating from rural Arkansas in the early 1800s to the cotton belt in the Mississippi Delta, the roots of the Berkeley family became known. Victims of the slave trade, the Berkeley family's roots were traced to large plantations where most had worked in fields planting, cultivating, and picking cotton; a few descendants had worked in homes cooking, cleaning, and nursing their slave owners' children.

Their status of slavery was not abolished until years after 1863, when President Lincoln's

Emancipation Proclamation declared slaves to be free in the Confederate States. After the Berkeley's were given freedom, they worked as sharecroppers on parcels of land where they grew cotton, corn, and other products. During the harvest time, they had to give the plantation owners half of what they earned from the sale of their crops. Because they operated with limited funds, the Berkeleys had to borrow money for survival. When their annual bills were paid, their debts were often greater than their income.

Offspring of the Berkeley roots grew impatient with living in sub-poverty conditions, and they began to migrate to other places.

During the Depression of the 1930s, many people were unemployed. Under the administration of President Franklin Delano Roosevelt, conservation projects were operating for young men and youth. From 1933 to 1942, the Civilian Conservation Corps (CCC) employed thousands of young men to live in camps for the protection and improvement of natural resources. Several young men from the Berkeley family were hired in this project, while others went to Chicago, Detroit, and other places to find employment. They shared their funds with family members who remained in Mississippi. This enabled them to pay off their debts and purchase forty acres of land and two mules to plow their crops.

Proliferation of the Berkeley family strengthened the support system. The life span of members became longer because younger members became health conscious and passed information on to older family members. Insurance companies were being operated by African-Americans for African-Americans, which made it possible for improved health care.

Schooling became available for more students, and the quality of education improved. The Berkeley family members pooled their resources whenever interest was shown in higher education. This made it possible for the number of educated family members to increase. When one achieved career goals, it was understood that others who were interested in higher education would be assisted.

MENTORSHIP WAS A WAY OF LIFE IN IMPROVING SOCIAL AND CULTURAL AWARENESS FOR THE BERKELEYS TO FIND NEEDS AND FILL THEM.

Mentorship was a way of life in improving social and cultural awareness for the Berkeleys to find needs and fill them. They were taught to utilize the scripture: "Ask, and it shall be given to you; seek, and you shall find; knock, and it shall be opened to you. For everyone who asks receives, and he who seeks finds, and to him who knocks it shall be opened" (Matt. 7:7–9 NASB).

Home and family influence continued to have high priority. In spite of the migration to many states in various career paths, the members came together annually in a reunion celebration at their home place in Mississippi. A structured program consisted of worshiping together regardless of diversified faiths, sharing their accomplishments, and planning for the future. Special programs were held for entertainment, talents, and hobbies, and were shared by all family members. Feasting and get-acquainted sessions strengthened the support system.

Career achievements were shared with goals and objectives outlined on both a long- and short-term basis. Workshops and lectures on various careers were given to inspire both young and old to increase their motivation to succeed. Ethical and spiritual values were shared with testimonies given to crystallize the importance of righteous living to enhance success in every area of life. Invitations were extended to mentors to share in culminating activities to express gratitude to those who had helped in providing support and positive reinforcement to the Berkeley family. Certificates of appreciation were awarded for jobs well done.

The primary goal for continuous growth of the Berkeley family in annual reunion meetings was achieved through the concerted efforts of all stake-holders in this family. As they reminisced about the past and shared their plans for a brighter future, they gave thanks for having a support system that was operational at all levels.

THE FELIX FAMILY
Experiencing Joy in Problem Solving

Surveys were sent annually to all Felix households to determine what problems they had encountered that could possibly be solved through group interaction. Recently, the highest priority was to celebrate a wedding of the oldest grandchild in the family. With limited budgets and distances to travel to a Central American city, the family had to plan how they could make the event a cherished memory for all members.

A planning committee representing all areas worked with the prospective bride and groom to plan for the total involvement of both sides of the families involved in the marriage. A checklist was made of needed human and material resources, and another checklist was made of talents and other competencies available in both families.

After the completion of both lists, they discovered that in the combined families they had all the resources needed to have an exemplary wedding. For example, they had a clergyman to perform the ceremony, musicians for vocal and instrumental music, a florist to provide flowers, attendants, a seamstress, a tailor, a caterer, a receptionist, a secretary, and travel agents. Members of the family volunteered their services for every area needed in planning and directing the wedding and sponsoring an outstanding reception.

Guest lists were prepared and reservations were made for a diversified group of people representing multicultural, multiethnic attendants. A total of over fifty had a joyful experience in celebrating the wedding and in coming together as a support system for two families blending into one healthy, happy, and terrific group focused on spreading joy and unconditional love for each other.

THE MATTHEWS FAMILY
Transforming Sadness into Gladness

A tragic automobile accident claimed the lives of both parents of the Matthews family, leaving four young children between the ages of one and fifteen. Without a will or instructions about their wishes in case of death, relatives were grief stricken and burdened in their bereavement. During a family meeting, the family survivors agreed that the four children should not be separated and should become an integral part of both surviving families. After much discussion, they decided that in order to have a strong support system for the young children, the maternal sister and her husband would become adopted parents and the other aunts and uncles would be the godparents.

With legal assistance, these arrangements were made. Ongoing psychological and social worker support helped with the comprehensive early childhood education program that was initiated.

Weekly contacts were made by the surviving relatives that provided support and positive reinforcement for each other. In spite of the grief that the children encountered, they were given an abundance of unconditional love and support from all family members. Help was available whenever they needed to solve any problem.

With the passing of time, the children and relatives on both sides of the surviving families grew closer to each other and cemented positive relationships, which elevated each child's self-esteem. The support system grew stronger and the evidence of bonding as a happy family became evident for the immediate and extended family members.

A time of grief resulted in the protection and love of the four young children and a cadre of caring, concerned, and committed adults whose unconditional love was visible in home, school, and community.

 JUAN AND ROXANNE
Expanding Social and Cultural Awareness in a Strong Support System

Having attended graduate school together in the United States, Juan and Roxanne developed a love affair that was going to be completed in marriage. Juan, a native of the British Virgin Islands, and Roxanne, a native of New York City, decided that there should be a cultural exchange between their

families and friends in order to develop an appreciation of the diversity in cultures and social
backgrounds and to develop cohesiveness as a
support system for their journey of matrimonial bliss.

They held weekly brainstorming sessions to
determine the best way to utilize workable strategies for bringing "togetherness" between the two
cultures. In an effort to develop a supportive atmosphere in their proposed wedding ceremony, they
agreed upon a plan.

Utilizing their knowledge, skills, and creativity
as journalism majors, they decided to write a
newsletter for family and friends as a travelogue
with significant stories about their plan to get
married. They included stories and pictures about
each country of origin as well as descriptions of
aspects of the Virgin Islands and the United States
that had impacted their lives.

Mailing lists of family members and friends
from both persons were compiled to receive a
monthly newsletter for the year prior to the
proposed wedding date. Each newsletter had a
space for readers to write questions about each
country that they wanted answered in follow-up
newsletters.

Subsequent newsletters had specific wedding
plans for the ceremony to be held in the Virgin
Islands during the summer, including a vacation
package plan that coincided with the wedding. A
follow-up one-year anniversary celebration
included a vacation plan in New York City. This

way, participants from both countries could cement their relationship and develop a support system. The plan worked with positive outcomes.

Family members and friends who traveled to both places increased their knowledge with first-hand information. Those who were unable to be involved in travel plans learned more about each country by reading the newsletters. Many who participated in the question and answer section gained additional knowledge.

Visions for developing bonds of friendship between the families and friends of Juan and Roxanne, through their creative approaches, widened the horizon of literacy and closed the gulf of diversity within their support systems of faith, hope, and unconditional love.

While they no longer send a newsletter monthly, they continue their publication on a semi-annual basis with news and pictures of themselves and other contributors in their support system.

Chapter Six

REFLECTIONS

 Reviewing the four examples of strong support systems shows that the challenges faced were different, but the basic needs were similar. Key terms in each support system were: *desire, dreams, daring,* and *determination.*

DESIRE

In each example, there was an expressed wish that underlined the submitted proposal. It was couched with an expression of hope that would result if the pieces of the puzzle's yearning could be put together in a pattern of reality.

DREAMS

Visualizing possibilities that could occur were the roots of possibilities in each example. Visions of the outcome in each example strengthened the imagination of solutions to the stated problems. As forerunners of reality, dreams provided provocative questions that led to a deepening of the "what if" principle.

COOPERATION AND COLLABORATION WERE INTEGRAL PARTS OF EACH SUPPORT SYSTEM.

DARING

Courage was evidenced as a result of becoming risk-takers who followed through on desires and dreams. Actions that were daring were proceeded with the affirmation "If at first you don't succeed, try, try again," and "nothing ventured, nothing gained."

DETERMINATION

Resolving to achieve predetermined goals was the core in the decision making process that amplified the determination to achieve. Cooperation and collaboration were integral parts of each support system: stakeholders planned, implemented, and monitored activities to ensure the successful conclusion in the achievement of goals and objectives as perceived by visionaries. The plans generated strong support systems as avenues for success in effective living and loving "self" and others, with caring, concerned, and committed minds, bodies, and souls.

SUPPORT SYSTEMS ARE STRENGTHENED

WHEN NEEDS ARE

COOPERATIVELY AND COLLABORATIVELY

IDENTIFIED AND MET.

Chapter Seven

A Bird's-Eye View of Support Systems in Action in South Africa

 During a recent educational tour of South and Southern Africa, our group had an opportunity to be in Durban at the beginning of the Thirteenth International Conference on Aids. Our tour guide explained the importance of support systems that work to solve problems in this continent, which is struggling to overcome the shackles of Apartheid that existed for years before the relatively new birth of democracy.

An impressive human-interest story captured our attention and illustrated that support systems are in action on a worldwide basis.

A white journalist adopted an illegitimate black orphan child after his mother died of AIDS. The journalist, along with others, formed a support system that gave the young boy tender, loving care and provided him with educational and cultural experiences that enabled him to overcome the deprivation he had suffered in his impoverished background.

His adopted mother selected the best school to enroll him in, to ensure excellence in teaching and learning. However, when parents and children discovered that this child was HIV positive, he met serious rejections that included the school administrator's decision to withdraw the child from this prestigious, predominantly white school and recommended that he transfer to an inner city school with substandard resources. Rejecting the school administrators' decision, the adopted mother secured a legal support system and took her case to court. She won the right for the child to remain in his school.

In spite of challenges, after a few years of schooling and enriching extra-curricular activities, the child became an excellent communicator with positive self-regard. He was invited to speak at the AIDS Conference about his story of overcoming numerous obstacles and succeeding in school as an honor student with a vocabulary that surpassed most students his age.

His support system continues to work and his future appears to be brighter because of one caring, concerned, and committed adult who changed the child's status from hopeless to hopeful.

While spending some time living in Swaziland, we stayed in Zululand. Many of the community people had little formal schooling. We were favorably impressed with one of our guides, a young Zulu woman who had grown up in the neighborhood and benefited from the support system of caring parents and others who financed her college education in Durban, South Africa, where she majored in drama. Returning to her home in Zululand, she was employed as a guide and as program coordinator for the Zulu's Activity Center.

These stories are examples of how a strong support system will enable one to overcome obstacles and to set and achieve goals for upward mobility in any place, at any time, and under any condition.

Another example of a support system in action was revealed in the interactions between members of our educational study tour in South Africa. Participants were from several states in various regions of the United States, with diversified backgrounds and different ages ranging from young adults to senior citizens.

A STRONG SUPPORT SYSTEM WILL ENABLE ONE TO OVERCOME OBSTACLES AND TO SET AND ACHIEVE GOALS FOR UPWARD MOBILITY IN ANY PLACE, AT ANY TIME, AND UNDER ANY CONDITION.

We formed a support system that enables our multicultural/multiethnic group to live harmoniously together for eighteen days in cities, villages, and campsites. Only a few of us knew each other prior to the trip; but we became a happy family of travelers with plans to continue our positive relationships. The success of our support system can be attributed to these actions:

- Getting to know and respect each other.
- Expressing unconditional love for each other.
- Communicating on a two-way basis with no put downs.
- Teaching and learning from each other.
- Giving and accepting constructive criticism.
- Using healthy humor to elevate morale.

Our daily activities were guided by the words in this poem by an unknown author:

Count your garden by the flowers
Never by the leaves that fall
Count your days by the golden hours
Don't remember clouds at all.
Count the nights by the stars
Not the shadows.
Count your life by smiles
Not by tears
And with joy on every birthday
Count your age by friends,
Not years.

A New Start

I will start anew this morning with a higher,
  fairer creed;
I will cease to stand complaining of my ruthless
  neighbor's greed;
I will cease to sit repining while my duty's call
  is clear;
I will waste no moment whining, and my
  heart shall know no fear.
I will look sometimes about me for the things
  that merit praise;
I will search for hidden beauties that elude the
  grumbler's gaze.
I will try to find contentment in the paths that
  I must tread;
I will cease to have resentment when another
  moves ahead.
I will not be swayed by envy when my rival's
  strength is shown;
I will not deny his merit, but I'll strive to prove
  my own;
I will try to see the beauty spread before me,
  rain or shine;
I will cease to preach your duty, and be more
  concerned with mine.

—Author Unknown

Chapter Eight

Suggestions for Developing a Support System for Excellence

Recognizing that support systems may be interpreted in different ways by different people, there is a thread of commonality that runs through every interpretation of the term. Data supporting the importance of unity of purpose in the identification of a team of people to build and maintain a foundation for success was repetitive. Describing basic ingredients of an effective support system were these terms: teamwork, teaching-learning, listening, problem solving, patience, understanding, sustaining faith, unconditional love, positive reinforcement, bridge-building, healthy self-esteem, responsiveness to unique needs, value, supportive relationships, and aspirations of self and others.

Quality of interaction, behavior modification as needed, and critical analysis are vital. Burden bearers, communicators, and positive thinkers who conceptualize, analyze, and report facts serve as advisors who give sincere, honest praise.

These ideas have worked for many who have been successful in developing effective support systems:

I *mage* the kind of support system that will meet your needs to succeed

D *evote* quality time and energy to recruiting, training, and supporting participants as supporters

E *nergize* yourself to work at strengthening your desire for a strong support system

A *ct* as if the support system is in operation

S *ell* your ideas to possible recruits for becoming a part of your system of support

F *ind* needs and fill them

O *rganize* your thoughts and actions

R *einforce* your thoughts and actions with positive reinforcement

D *irect your actions* with the end results in mind

E *xpect the best* from each member of your support team

V *alue the contributions* of all members

E *ngage in daily conversation* and problem-solving strategies

L *ove each person* unconditionally

O *bey the commands* of success

P *lan, and work* the plan

I *nitiate creative approaches* to problem solving

N *urture the suggestions* of others and utilize them to strengthen your support system

G *ive freely* to lift others as you climb the ladder of success

A *dvance your progress* on a daily basis

S *earch for new ideas* to grow

U *nderstand others* during communication

P *ackage your potential* to help others

P *ray for guidance*

O *pen opportunities* for team members to grow

R *ecognize the strengths* of others and cultivate them

T *each others* what you have learned

S *avor your achievement* with celebrations of your success

Y *ield not* to the temptation to sin

S *ee the good* in others and give sincere, honest praise

T *hank each membe*r of your support system for steps of improvement

E *njoy* your team

M *eet deadlines* for action plans

F *ollow through* on goals to achieve your fondest dreams

O *rder your steps* in terms of priority to maintain a state of harmony

R *adiate your personality* to manifest a friendly disposition

E *xpand your point of view* to increase the scope of your effectiveness

X *ray your vision* and mission to determine the impact of your goals

C *ommit to journal writing* every day

E *xercise your mind, body, and soul* regularly for the sake of training and improvement

L *ead others* in setting and achieving precedents in maintaining a positive influence

L *eave a legacy of faith,* hope, and love for future generations

E *ducate self and others* for edifying knowledge, morals, and faith

N *egotiate* to reach agreements

C *onnect with a Higher Power* to ensure success

E *ase anxiety* with positive actions

Chapter Nine

STRONG SUPPORT SYSTEMS

 Guideposts for planning, implementing, and maintaining the avenues of success for strong support systems are erected as facilitators for comprehensive services in the process of training. Preventive and corrective services modify behaviors, habits, and mental attitudes to ensure the attainment of fixed purpose of operation.

Ingredients for making, monitoring, protecting, and coordinating systems as avenues of success are included in these components:

S tress is placed on finding needs and filling them.

T rust is involved in developing positive relationships.

R einforcement and resiliency are encouraged.

O utcomes of activities are visualized.

N eeds for improvement are addressed.

G rowth is continuous for personal development.

S ervice is provided for positive reinforcement.

U nity of purpose is encouraged.

P lans are made to set and achieve goals.

P atience is practiced in teaching and learning.

O bjectives are specific in goal setting and decision-making.

R esources are made available for meeting needs and interests.

T raining is continuous for career development choices.

S kills are developed for self-directed learning.

Y outh and adult mentorship programs are continuous for self-improvement.

S elf-acceptance, self-confidence, self-control, and self-worth activities are ongoing.

T ime management for success is practiced.

E nhancement of strengths to cope with challenges in lifelong learning is practiced.

M anagement of human and material resources generates positive outcomes.

S elf-evaluation of goals and objectives assess effectiveness of efforts.

PHYSICAL DEVELOPMENT

By training physical bodies and providing activities to give strength and support for the collective whole, capable people are produced to function in productive ways.

INTELLECTUAL DEVELOPMENT

Exercising mental faculties in creative and critical thinking demands that intellectual interests operate for the best interests of the group in setting and achieving the mind power necessary to make systems work effectively.

SOCIAL AND CULTURAL AWARENESS

Living, working, and interacting in friendly relationships promotes unity of purpose. Strong support systems evolve from the ability to cope with mutual goals and an understanding of the end results. Multicultural/multiethnic understanding of the importance of diversity in building support systems enhances the growth and development of varied systems.

HOME AND FAMILY INFLUENCE

Units of parents and children function as structures of support for each other. Extension of these units, such as friends, provide unconditional love to further the interests and regard for each other. Thus, the home, workplace, and school, as well as community activities, influence each other and heighten the power of human interaction to produce high achievers.

ETHICAL AND SPIRITUAL VALUES

Right conduct and practices are attributes of members of a strong support system. "Inner-winning" principles activate soul-stirring beliefs in the sacredness of the power of an effective system of believers to be a guiding force of influence.

CAREER DEVELOPMENT

Professional growth and development propels support systems of people to draw out the best in themselves through education in professions that are geared toward meeting their unique needs and interests. Vocations of specialized training in diversified fields adds to the competencies of the support system.

FINANCIAL MANAGEMENT

The process of producing and consuming fiscal resources helps avoid extravagance and adds to the fiscal health of the economic system. Safeguarding funds and making wise investments helps in the enhancement of independent living in strong support systems. Words of encouragement with guidance in the graduation, distribution, and management of finances gives incentives for working effectively to strengthen and reinforce goal setting and decision making.

Strong support systems are not satisfied with maintaining excellence only in their fields of operation. Instead, they generate opportunities in mentorship programs that replicate their success in all areas. Their self-esteem as a system is healthy and free of egotism because they operate under these guiding principles:

- *Self-Acceptance*—Each person is recognized as a contributing member of society. Each one accepts himself or herself as a biological wonder created in the image of a Supreme Being.
- *Self-Respect*—Each member is held in high regard and operates on the honor code of the Golden Rule of conduct.
- *Self-Control*—Each member exercises restraint in actions, reactions, and interactions. Each practices this affirmation of St. Francis of Assisi: "God grant me the serenity to accept things I cannot change, the courage to change things I can, and the wisdom to know the difference."
- *Self-Confidence*—Each member has self-reliance and a belief in his or her ability to find needs and fill them. This is the hallmark of approval of faith in the trust and capability of performance.
- *Self-Worth*—Each member understands that his or her value cannot be measured and that value is a priceless, esteemed internal gift.

These are positive images that empower participants in a strong support system to soar like eagles,
overcoming adversities that deter success, and
transforming obstacles into opportunities to
succeed. These images give support to the meek,
upward mobility to the downcast, and faith to
doubters. They provide the water of life to prime
the pump of despair, and a castle of hope in the
dungeon of hopeless unbelievers.

Chapter Ten

CONCLUSIONS

 All of the evidence collected from my experiences and research overwhelmingly proves my conviction that strong support systems are avenues for success.

Results of the interviews I have conducted conclude that these guideposts contribute to the success of a group's support system.

In the strong support systems I have encountered, the major players in the development of each system were immediate and extended family members, members representing diversified careers, friends, and positive reinforcers with visionary

G *uidance and support* of caring, concerned, and committed supporters

U *nderstanding the unique needs* and interests of each team member

I *nvolvement of all supporters* in planning, implementing, and monitoring all activities

D *evotion to the goals and objectives* of the group

E *valuation* of program outcomes

P *rioritization of programs* to be implemented

O *rganization of mission* and visions of the support system

S *elf-fulfillment* of personalized and group goals

T *eamwork* in making the support system effective

S *cripting the spiritual* journey of success

competencies. In each support system, career paths were chosen that identified specific needs and interests. Visions were generated at different stages and ages of life whenever there was a visible need that could be met by a designated group within a designated time frame. Concerted efforts were made to engage in decision making and goal setting to pinpoint progress at various points and to plan to pass the torch of success to others in succeeding generations.

Looking back, assessing the present, and looking forward to the future all reveal that daily survival comes from the support and positive reinforcement of numerous support systems.

Recently, while I was visiting family members in a midwestern city, I had a visit from the pastor of a local church. I had known him since he was a freshman in college. When I shared with him the manuscript for this book, he commented that he had not only been thinking about the advantages of a strong support system but had preached about it in one of his weekly sermons. He said it had generated positive feedback. The title of the sermon was "Standing on Someone's Shoulders."

Briefly, he shared how civilization evolved as followers stood on the shoulders of leaders who made it possible for them to succeed. Using several stories in biblical history, he showed how ancient Hebrews survived the suffering of slavery, crossed through the wilderness of despair, drank from streams that quenched bodies almost dead from thirst, and ate miraculous food to ease the pains of hunger—all because they stood on the shoulders of exemplary leaders who had the spiritual power to communicate with their Supreme Being.

He shared that he had a small biological family and an enormous extended family system of students, teachers, members of his faith organization, fraternity members, and others. He was able to achieve both long- and short-range goals because he was able to stand on many shoulders.

After graduation from college, he became an officer in the U.S. Army, got married, had two daughters, traveled to many states and countries, and experienced success in his military career—all because strong shoulders made it possible for him to stand up and overcome the obstacles that often clouded his future.

After an honorable discharge from the army, he joined the corporate world and earned a large salary to support himself and his family. Reflecting on life's journey of standing on the shoulders of others, he made the decision to prepare for ministry. By becoming the pastor of a church, he believes that he is providing shoulders for many of his parishioners to stand. This is his way of giving thanks and developing support systems to replicate his blessings as he reaches for new heights in building stronger support systems for success.

After listening and reacting to this pastor's words of wisdom, I was moved to enumerate how my support system has operated for many decades.

Jotting them in a journal became an endless task because the number grew larger and larger as I categorized each support system that operated in home, school, workplace, and in faith and community organizations.

Positive reinforcement came from many sources to help build my support systems. One reinforcement I vividly recall from early childhood was hearing groups of sharecroppers in the cotton fields singing spirituals. One song was a soul-stirring message of faith, hope, and unconditional love that said: "Father, I stretch my hands to thee, no other help I know. If thou withdraw thyself from me, oh whither shall I go."

Those sharecroppers were visionaries who knew the value of a strong support system and could affirm that "where there is vision, there is hope; where there is hope, there is faith; and where there is faith, there is love."

SUGGESTIONS

Keep a daily journal of your support system for at least a month. Make entries of the support systems you enjoy in these areas:

HOME

_____

_____

_____

_____

_____

_____

_____

_____

_____

SCHOOL

_____

_____

_____

_____

_____

_____

WORKPLACE

_____

_____

_____

_____

_____

_____

ORGANIZATIONS

_____

_____

_____

_____

_____

_____

RECREATION

_____

_____

_____

_____

_____

_____

OTHER

_____

_____

_____

_____

_____

_____

Give Thanks For Everything

NOTES

1. Frank J. Sparzo, *The ABC's of Behavior Change* (Bloomington, In.: Phi Delta Kappa International Inc., 1999).

2. Ibid., 63.

3. Sirgay Sanger and John Kelly, *The Woman Who Works, the Parent Who Cares* (Boston: Kittle Brown & Co., 1987).

4. Katherine Schlaerth, *Raising a Large Family* (New York: Macmillian Publishing Co., 1991).

5. Nancy Samalin, *Loving Your Child Is Not Enough— Positive Discipline that Works* (New York: Viking, 1987), 187.

6. Ibid., 209.

7. Thomas Paris and Eileen Paris, *I'll Never Do to My Kid What My Parents Did to Me* (Chicago: Contemporary Books, 1992).

8. Ibid., 142–43.

9. Ruth Peters, *Don't Be Afraid to Discipline* (New York: Golden Books, 1997), 30.

10. Stephen R. Covey, *The 7 Habits of Highly Effective People* (New York: Simon & Schuster, 1989), 283.

11. Lawrence J. Greene, *1001 Ways to Improve Your Child's School Work* (New York: Dell, 1991), 17.

12. Ibid., 267.

13. Stephanie Marston, *The Magic of Encouragement* (New York: William Marrow, 1990).

14. Walter Barbe, *Growing Up Learning* (Washington D.C.: Acropolis Books, 1985).

15. Charles Schaefer, *How to Influence Children,* 2d ed. (New York: Van Nostrand Reinhold Co., 1982), 41.

16. Ibid, 268–69.

17. Theodore Isaac Rubin, *Child Potential* (New York: Continuum Publishing Co., 1990), 289.

18. Ibid.

19. Schaefer, 233.

20. Ibid., 234.

21. Susan Crites Price and Tom Price, *The Working Parents' Help Book* (Princeton, N.J.: Peterson's 1994).

22. James McBride, *The Color of Water: A Black Man's Tribute to His White Mother* (New York: Riverhead Books, 1996).

23. Virgie Binford, *Climbing the Success Ladder: The Ten Commandments of Effective Parent Education Performance* (Richmond, Va.: Barnett, 1985).

24. Ibid, 62–63.

25. Ibid., 35–47.

26. Horace Mann, "The Ground of the Free School System" in *Old South Leaflets* Vol. 5, No. 109 (Boston, Mass.: Directors of Old South Work, 1902), 108.

27. "Panel Report V of the Special Studies Project of Rockefeller Brothers' Fund, Inc." in *The Pursuit of Excellence in Education and the Future of America* (Garden City, N.Y.: Doubleday and Co., Inc., 1958), 1–49.

BIBLIOGRAPHY

Barbe, Walter. *Growing Up Learning.* Washington, D.C.: Acropolis Books, 1985.

Binford, Virgie. *Climbing the Success Ladder: The Ten Commandments of Effective Parent Education Performance.* Richmond, Va.: Barnett, 1985.

Covey, Stephen R. *The 7 Habits of Highly Effective People.* New York: Simon & Schuster, 1989.

Greene, Lawrence. *1001 Ways to Improve Your Child's School Work.* New York: Dell, 1991.

Marston, Stephanie. *The Magic of Encouragement.* New York: William Marrow, 1990.

McBride, James. *The Color of Water: A Black Man's Tribute to His White Mother.* New York: Riverhead Books, 1996.

Paris, Thomas and Eileen Paris. *I'll Never Do to My Kids What My Parents Did to Me.* Chicago: Contemporary Books, 1992.

Peters, Ruth. *Don't Be Afraid to Discipline.* New York: Golden Books, 1997.

Price, Susan Crites and Tom Price. *The Working Parents' Help Book.* Princeton, N.J.: Peterson's, 1994.

Rubin, Theodore Isaac. *Child Potential.* New York: Continuum Pub. Co., 1990.

Samalin, Nancy. *Loving Your Child Is Not Enough—Positive Discipline that Works.* New York: Viking, 1987.

Sanger, Sirgay and John Kelly. *The Woman Who Works, the Parent Who Cares.* Boston: Kittle Brown & Co., 1987.

Schaefer, Charles. *How to Influence Children.* 2d ed. New York: Van Nostrand Reinhold Co, 1982.

Schlaerth, Katherine. *Raising a Large Family.* New York: Macmillan Pub. Co., 1991.

Sparzo, Frank. *The ABC's of Behavior Change.* (Bloomington, In.: Phi Delta Kappa International, Inc., July, 1999).

"Here are children in need and must be helped."
                                    —NELSON MANDELA

The above statement by the former president of
South Africa, Nelson Mandela, is his justification of
why he started a children's fund in his name in 1994.
According to one of his biographers, Mandela gave
one-third of his annual salary as "a way to change
how society treats children." He continued by stating
that raising funds is a huge task that requires time,
constant dedication, energy, and money for achieving
excellence for children (Published in *South Africa
Information for Hotel Guests*).

ABOUT THE AUTHOR

VIRGIE M. BINFORD is an educational consultant, motivational speaker, and workshop facilitator. She serves on the executive board of directors of the National Council on Self-Esteem. A graduate of Virginia State University, Binford earned her bachelor's and master's degrees in elementary education before earning her doctorates at Virginia Tech and New Hope Bible College and Seminary. She has studied at Columbia University and has furthered her education at the University of Virginia and in international studies. Binford served Richmond Public Schools as a teacher, supervisor, and director of various education programs. She is an adjunct instructor at J. Sargeant Reynolds Community College and has previously taught at Virginia Union University. Binford is actively involved in civic, church, and educational organizations, including the National Coalition of 100 Black Women, All Souls Presbyterian Church, and Pi Lambda Theta.